ANGELIC LUMINOSITIES

ORBS, LIGHT WAVES, LIGHT RODS & OTHER INTERDIMENSIONAL SPIRIT BEINGS

AuthorHouse™ LLC
1663 Liberty Drive
Bloomington, IN 47403
www.authorhouse.com
Phone: 1-800-839-8640

© 2014 Angelique Patrice. All rights reserved.

No part of this book may be reproduced, stored in a retrieval system,
or transmitted by any means without the written permission of the author.

Published by AuthorHouse 03/19/2014

ISBN: 978-1-4918-3991-1 (sc)
978-1-4918-6110-3 (e)

Any people depicted in stock imagery provided by Thinkstock are models,
and such images are being used for illustrative purposes only.
Certain stock imagery © Thinkstock.

This book is printed on acid-free paper.

Because of the dynamic nature of the Internet, any web addresses or links contained in this book may have changed since publication and may no longer be valid. The views expressed in this work are solely those of the author and do not necessarily reflect the views of the publisher, and the publisher hereby disclaims any responsibility for them.

ANGELIC LUMINOSITIES
ORBS, LIGHT WAVES, LIGHT RODS & OTHER INTERDIMENSIONAL SPIRIT BEINGS

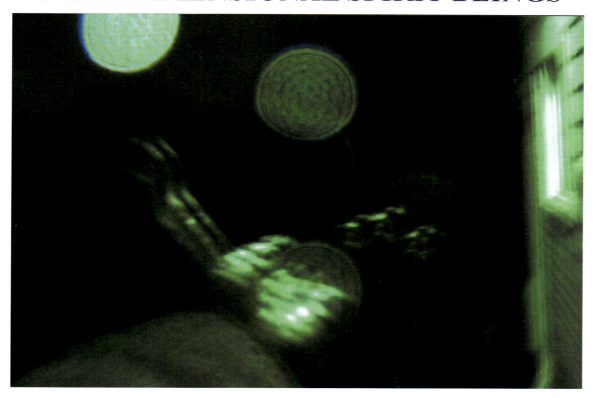

ANGELIQUE PATRICE

CONTENTS

INTRODUCTION vii

INTERDIMENSIONAL LIGHT BEINGS 1

MAGNIFICENT, MYSTERIOUS SPHERES OF LIGHT 5

ORBS, LUMINOUS BEINGS OF THE NIGHT 8

ENERGY IN VARIOUS FORMS AND COLORS 22

LIGHT RODS 32

SEGMENTED WORMS 36

LIGHT WAVES 48

BEAUTIFUL ENERGY FORMATIONS 60

Closing Thoughts 80

Author Bio 82

INTRODUCTION

In "Angelic Luminosities" you will see Spirit Beings delivering messages with various formations as well as showing their love. These intelligent Beings, through photos taken of them, actually show that communication is possible.

Also evident is their heart-felt, fun loving nature that will mesmerize the very soul of your Being, and inspire you to open your mind to new realms of existence. Learn how you may be able to interact with these multi-dimensional Beings.

The front cover picture shows my hand being penetrated by an Orb after I asked it to come into my hand while shooting pictures one evening. This was the beginning of a fascinating communication that I developed through many nights of photographing Orbs, Light Waves, Light Rods, and Segmented Worms, including other luminous Beings now coming into the Earth plane.

I hope to encourage others to become interested in learning what messages these Light Beings would like to share that may possibly help us understand more about the Hidden Realms.

INTERDIMENSIONAL LIGHT BEINGS

In this life we all have a calling or purpose for being here. Some of us find out what we are meant to do at an early age while others finally figure it out later on in life. At long last I've found my passion. Nothing excites my soul more than taking photos of these beautiful Light Beings that are coming into this realm. Their presence shows us that many kinds of life exist in other dimensions and there is so much more to behold than just life on this planet.

Anyone with a camera and an open mind with good intention can get pictures of Orbs and other various inter-dimensional beings. My desire now is merely to share these experiences with others of interest and possibly to open the minds of those having a skeptical nature about the paranormal.

In case you are wondering how or why I began getting these particular kinds of pictures, though now many people do, it's much more than just taking photos. It has to do with a unique inner feeling and desire to know what these beautiful spheres of light are and how we relate to each other. I wanted to know why they are appearing in so many pictures and what they are trying to communicate to us.

One afternoon I was having lunch with a girl friend, and being an accomplished photographer, she brought her $1200 Nikon along to take pictures for her scrap book. After taking some photos, we looked at the pictures of me and there were Orbs shown through the sunlight coming from a window behind me. They were all around my head and shoulders. How cool, I could hardly believe my eyes.

Though oddly enough, the Orbs were not in the pictures of my friend for whatever reason, only pictures of me. So I decided to change places with her, having her sit in front of that same window with the sun light coming through. But there were no Orbs in those pictures either. After exchanging cameras and taking several more shots, it was obvious that the Orbs were not showing up around her even with the expensive Nikon. They were only in the pictures of me taken with my Olympus. Curiously I wanted to know why; later I would find out.

It is my understanding that it depends on the energy vibration of the one shooting the pictures as to whether or not they attract Orbs, but one must be consistent not giving up too easily. These Beings have to slow their vibration down in order to stay here awhile. Some of the pictures even show some double exposure because of their higher frequency.

From that day on my Olympus became my constant companion helping me escape from a rather boring life style I had gotten accustomed to after the passing of my soul mate husband in 2006. I was starting to become a hermit; staying home most of the time, grieving my loss and only going out for necessities and an occasional lunch with a girl friend. Unfortunately, this went on for about three years.

I had started taking pictures right outside my house photographing many large white Orbs with patterns, and beautiful Light Waves or Plasma. As I could not physically see them, it was very hard to get more than one or two shots at a time. The Light Waves kept moving to the right so I had to keep turning, slowly, constantly shooting as fast as the camera would allow, trying to capture their essence before they disappeared back into infinity. At times, I even aimed the camera straight up into the sky where Light Waves were moving up above my head. Wherever I pointed the lens, they appeared. I soon came to realize these waves of energy had their own purpose for coming into the photos.

Oh how fascinated and inspired I was that my life once again was being led down this metaphysical path in which I had before been involved for several years. A feeling of passion had been rekindled that I never would have thought possible. Shooting, deleting, cropping to show more detail, and printing the pictures had become a full time hobby and at the same time was also turning into a spiritual quest helping me move on from loneliness and grief to an exciting new realm of possibilities.

In my amazement upon receiving all these photos of the Beings, I began taking hundreds of pictures night after night. You could say it actually became an obsession. After each shooting, I would go through and delete any pictures without Orbs or with Beings that were too far away. Then I would go back outside and continue on. It became very time consuming some nights, but well worth the effort. Spiritual Beings of Light bringing in Love for you and me to experience.

The Veil is Lifting!!!

At the Light Workers meeting I attend once a month, we share spiritual experiences and discuss whatever insights we believe will raise not only our vibration, but the vibration of all life. This special, loving group has been instrumental in my spiritual growth and with them I am always able to share my photos. They help me interpret the meanings of some of the pictures and continue to always be supportive and inspiring to be around. All of them have their own special gifts to share and more love than you can imagine for all life on this planet and beyond.

About two years ago I was told there is a portal or entrance outside my house which allows Beings from other dimensions to come through into this realm. I have been so blessed to receive some photos that are almost unbelievable and this portal may be the reason why I get so many different varieties. Also, several years ago, I asked Spirit or God (whichever you prefer) to help me make a difference and to show me that it does actually exist. For me, these pictures are part of my answer to those wishes.

My mother has been my main guru in life turning me on to many great books and authors through the years, always allowing her children to choose their own belief system, and encouraging them to keep an open mind. She is now 86 years young and still works at a co-op, and reads books on Quantum Physics, Consciousness and Alternative Health. Being very well read and devoted to learning about enlightenment her whole life, she should be writing her own life story. It would be a great read, I am sure.

MAGNIFICENT, MYSTERIOUS SPHERES OF LIGHT

Orbs come in many shapes and colors. The very large white Orbs often have patterns in them. Others appear in all colors of the rainbow including the actual color of gold or they may be multi-colored. Through these past years of working with them and establishing some communication, it is my opinion that the large white Orbs may be people that have passed on and have gone to the light or possibly the Orb is the energy vehicle the spirit uses to travel throughout the Cosmos. They are different from spirits that have chosen to stay here on the Earth plane whom have been labeled ghosts. Just thinking of our past loved ones will bring them close, for they know our thoughts and we are never really alone.

There are Orbs that appear to have human faces in them while others have what look like animal faces, usually being a cat or dog and some are perfectly round while others are oval shaped. Yet at other times, they appear as pentagrams, hexagons, triangles or octagon shapes – even heart shapes showing love and are basically able to take on any form they wish. Some will appear as spheres and in the next picture they have all changed to pentagrams and then back to spheres again in the following pictures. While continuously shooting, they move and may appear in a different place in two or three pictures taken consecutively.

If it is your desire to communicate with the Orbs and Light Waves, just ask a question while taking pictures and you may be shown the answer. Your intention will be known instantly as these Light Beings are able to read your energy and thoughts. Most likely they will not appear in your pictures if you are a skeptic, unless you are open to learning what they have to teach. Then they will take you places beyond your normal perception of reality. You won't have to travel far to get their pictures, they will come to you. If they want to be around your energy, they will.

I have learned to keep my camera close for it has my energy on it. Someone else may use it and get very few if any Orb photos, yet that same person may get many using their own camera because it has their energy on it. Possibly, each of us attracts certain Beings – whichever Beings help with our spiritual growth or resonate with our energy. Some people may work with Angels and others with Orbs or other Light Beings. I believe we all have Guardian Angels and Guides that are always helping us along our path and I would never rule out the possibility of Alien Beings from other dimensions also appearing as Orbs.

There is nothing to fear from Orbs, Light Waves, Light Rods, Segmented Worms or other luminous beings you will see in these photos. Orbs are pure energy which have an aura, as we do, and are just as interested in us as we are in them. You will be able to see how some of these Light Beings express themselves in the following pictures and how they love to play and have a sense of humor.

Light Rods are pure white energy and it is said they may get their energy from electrical wires, lights and storms. They are able to go right through you or anything for that matter, and they may help with spiritual development if you ask them. None of these Beings project a negative energy, only loving, helpful energy. At least this is the feeling I get when taking pictures though I never focus on darkness. Perhaps what you focus on is what you get. You can always surround yourself with white light from the Universe for protection if you feel the need.

It is my belief we are here to learn unconditional love for all life and we are all ONE, just different frequencies. If we will only let go of judgment and develop unconditional love for all life, what a peaceful, loving world it would be. Is it possible for us, together, to create a better world? I believe as we raise our consciousness, all life everywhere will benefit.

Lately peculiar things have been happening. I started seeing the Light Waves in my peripheral vision moving to my upper left while looking straight ahead taking the photo. Before I could only see the Light Waves after the picture was taken. I also see moving waves of energy in my peripheral vision while reading at night.

Several times now when I look up at the Sun it turns bright red and is constantly breathing or pulsating. After that, sometimes it changes to silver and back to red again. Then a bright yellow color appears all around the outside. It is so amazingly beautiful. No, I don't take any drugs – not even prescription drugs. Our lives are so busy now it seems we often don't take the time to see the beauty in nature. If we slow down and appreciate its beauty, who knows what we may be shown.

Most of the following pictures were taken at night with flash in Washington and Oregon. I do, sometimes get Orbs and other Beings without flash but I think the flash helps attract them. None of these pictures have been altered in any way, only cropped to block out the background and to bring the Light Beings up closer allowing more detail to be seen. The opinions and information are based on my experiences throughout the past six years and many years of continued interest in paranormal phenomena.

Some of you will be awed and flabbergasted, as I was. I surely hope so. Others unfortunately, distraught with disbelief. It's difficult for some to believe in the unknown or anything they can't physically see. Though there are many things on this Earth we know exist but we cannot see with the naked eye. What about the vastness of the many universes and multiple dimensions? I doubt we could ever behold all the life that exists out there in space during one lifetime.

Enjoy.

ORBS, LUMINOUS BEINGS OF THE NIGHT

Large white Orbs linger around my house at night. Here you can see two Orbs overlapping each other. I have learned from my dear cousin that passed on in 2012 that these are two souls that were very connected here on Earth, probably a man and wife or long time friends.

These Orbs have a blue/purple aura on one side and a yellow/green aura on the other. Most have a pattern in them and some have faces. Recently I saw UFO's on a web site that also have auras of the same colors. ***Coincidence?***

While having lunch, I told my friend that I couldn't believe the Orbs were here for me. Why were they surrounding me? Obviously hearing what I said, one Orb planted itself right on my face, showing me it was going to get my attention.

Just can't get away with nothin!!!

After being told that Light Waves/Plasma are hundreds of Orbs – I, myself, was skeptical. While taking this picture I asked the question, "Are you really a bunch of Orbs?" In response, the Light Waves showed me a string of Plasma forming Orbs.

Ask and You Shall Receive!

After I learned that I was able to communicate with some of the Orbs while taking their pictures, I asked one to come into my hand. Surprisingly, it did.

Look at the pattern on these. Perhaps they all have their own, unique pattern.

Beautiful Rose Pink Orbs, connected at the side. In understanding that the large white Orbs connected at top and bottom were together in their lifetime on Earth as partners, I wondered if the Orbs that are connected at the side, as these two pink Orbs are, may have been siblings or possibly twins here on Earth.

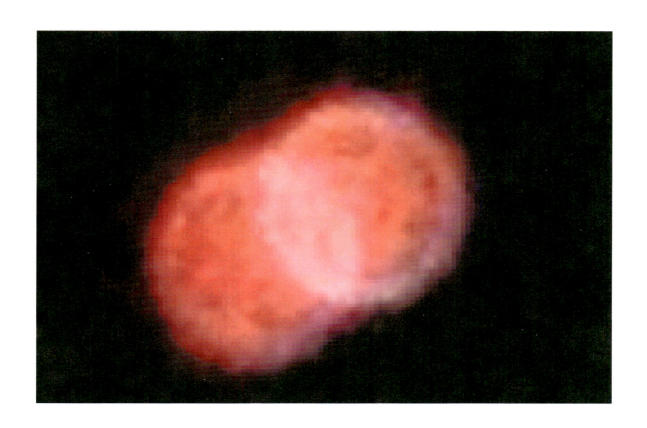

Mom's husband passed on in 2004 but we knew he was still around her. I told her to focus on him and while taking her pictures I asked him if he would let her know that he was still alive and well by giving her a big kiss. **Lovingly, he did.**

Our passed loved ones want us to be happy and want us to know they are ok. I think it is possible for them to be in multiple places at the same time. That way they can be in another realm or dimension learning whatever the soul needs to learn and at the same time be visiting loved ones on the Earth plane. They are unlimited multi-dimensional Beings.

ENERGY IN VARIOUS FORMS AND COLORS

This misty green energy ball appeared in several places around my front yard. It also made an appearance a few times after that night. Green energy is healing.

This soft pink energy has appeared for several pictures. When I asked it to come closer to my hand, it did. In a few other pictures it appeared on my hand. Pink energy means **LOVE.**

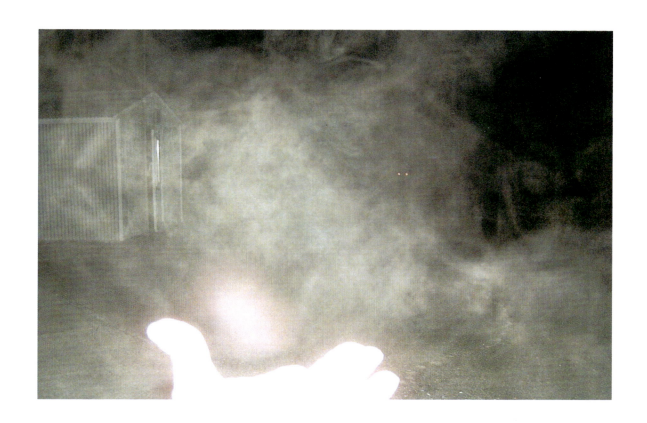

Energy penetrating my hand with some double exposure from the higher frequency. **Spooky!!!**

These mist like energy balls appeared one late afternoon before dark. As I kept shooting pictures they moved to the right in several places around the yard.

This Energy Ball moved up on the wire showing a **Being** in its Center.

Rising up higher, this energy playfully formed a doughnut in the sky. Excited, I ran to the back yard consistently shooting pictures and the energy moved across the lawn in front of me and then went back up into the sky and formed another doughnut.

Simply Fascinating!!!

I began getting these kinds of pictures in 2006 shortly after my husband's passing. These Spirit Beings are the very reason I started coming out of my grief and depression, though slowly. Now I know that was part of their purpose for coming into my life – to lift me up by expressing their Light, Love and Beauty. I feel so blessed and look forward to learning all I can about their presence here.

LIGHT RODS

A Light Rod poses in my living room. You can see how the room has some double exposure but the Light Rod, itself, does not. The Rod has to slow its frequency to stay in one place for the picture and temporarily remain here in this dimension.

A Light Rod outside of my house looking in. See how much double exposure the house shows.

Not sure if this is a Light Rod or an Orb leaving a trail along its path to other realms. Doesn't quite look like an Orb trail, or a Light Rod. Bet it's a new Being wanting to get its photo in this book.

SEGMENTED WORMS

Pink, Green and Blue Segmented Worms streaming through the night sky in Oregon, perhaps on their way to Never Land?

I was curious to see if I could communicate with Segmented Worms also. While taking pictures, I asked this Green Segmented Worm if it would wrap itself around the tree in the back yard. Guess what? As you can see, it let me know they also are intelligent Beings that can hear our thoughts and want to communicate with us.

Following it was this Golden Segmented Worm being a copy cat. They do like to show off at times.

My Golden Point Siamese happened to be standing by the tree, so I then asked the Segmented Worm to wrap itself around the cat. While shooting the pictures, Casper started walking toward me and the next picture showed this Golden Worm along side of him disappearing into the ground. Wonder if the cat can see them.

My son, who has always been a bit skeptical, stood outside with these friendly Segmented Worms keeping him company. Little did he know they were there, right beside him.

My grandson, on the left, was standing in the road as I took this picture with all this energy surrounding him. A psychic friend of mine said there are several musical instruments in this energy – one being a piano. I wonder if this means he may have the ability to play a variety of musical instruments.

Here is a little different form of the Segmented Worm. I asked this one to come closer, and it did. Love to get their picture taken.

LIGHT WAVES

These Light Waves make up an obvious face with large eyes. Perhaps it could be some Beings I knew in another realm of existence coming to visit. In the upper left it looks like another face also.

These may be thousands of Orbs traveling together. Wonder how many different dimensions they visit in a night.

Beautiful Waves of Pink, Blue, and Green Light. I love it when they express a variety of colors. Must be their aura colors.

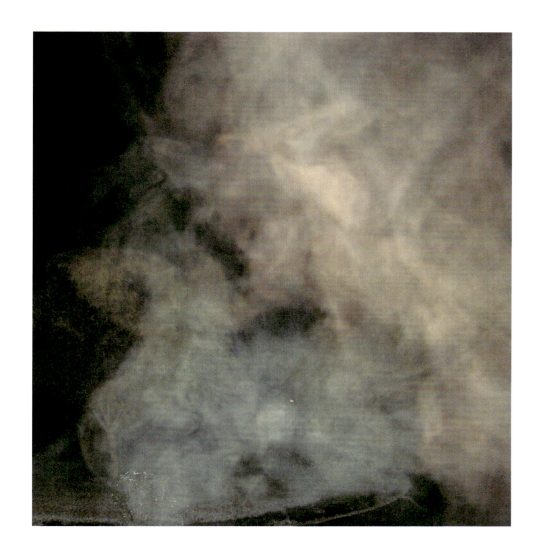

Light Waves with pretty little pink and blue Orbs.

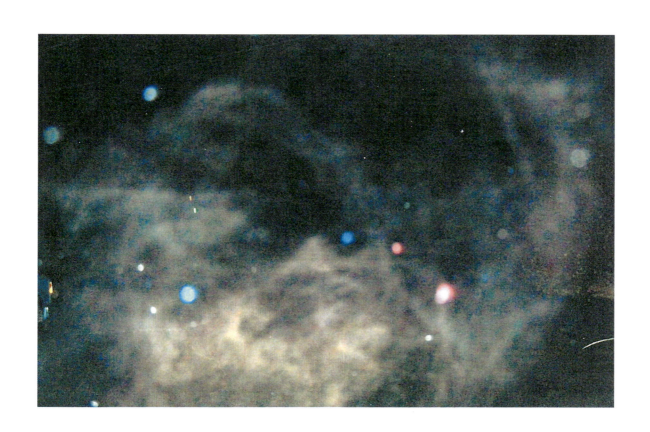

Unknowingly surrounded by Light Waves, my lovely daughter gets ready to leave while a large white Orb to the far left looks on. Of course my two children think I am weird, out taking pictures of things I don't see. But I think they are the ones missing out on all the fun.

My brother came to stay the night a couple of years ago and after going to the small bedroom to retire, the light started flickering on and off, but not at the light bulb area, up higher at the top of the bulb – the part that screws into the light fixture. Strangely enough though – the light wasn't even turned on. This happened a few more times and he called out for me to come quickly. I went to the room and the light flickered on and off again a few more times. We looked at the light switch and it was in the off position. I was excited and thought it was cool.

Well my brother never would sleep in the small bedroom after that. He decided to camp out on the couch instead. I think it's kind of funny and I tease him about it whenever he comes over. But he thinks my house is haunted. I told him it's probably just dad trying to communicate with him but he still doesn't know what to think.

Guess nothing surprises me. I know Light Rods and other Spirit Beings go through the house all the time. With the veil lifting, we may soon be able to see many of these Beings without the camera. Wouldn't that be delightful?

One evening a good friend was getting ready to leave and her whole car was over taken by Light Waves. Wonder if they followed her home that night.

This was taken as my sweet granddaughter waits for her taxi. It's a good thing most people can't see these Light Waves, otherwise it could be rather frightening.

BEAUTIFUL ENERGY FORMATIONS

At first I thought this looked like an Angel's wing in my living room. But my psychic friend said there are three dolphins (their noses on the lower left) swimming in this picture.

Some people are able to see things others can't or won't see. I hope to enhance this ability so I will always be able to understand what messages these Light Beings are trying to reveal.

My psychic friend said this is an Angel facing the tree. You can see the wings folded back. In the upper left hand corner an Orb takes flight.

Quite exciting to see this Blue String Being gliding along in the dark. I call this beautiful Being **"The Blue Glider."**

The same **Blue Glider with a little Red Dragon** on its back. It is said Fairies and Dragons among other Beings, have come back into this realm again.

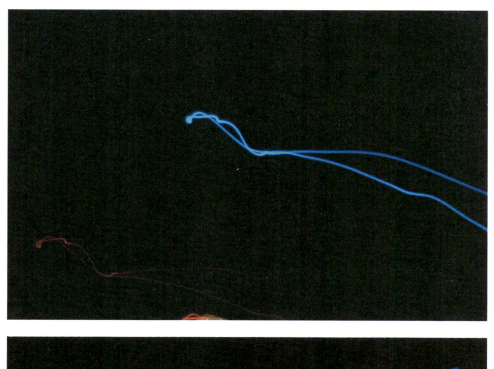
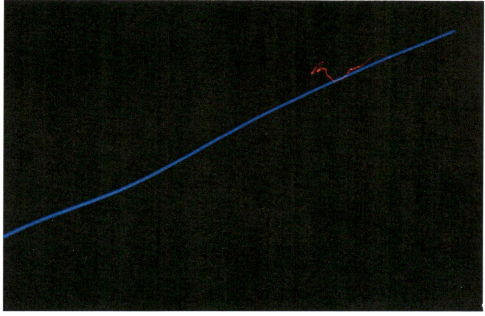

I call these Segmented Worms, **"Dancers in the Night"**. They love to play.   What Show Offs!!!

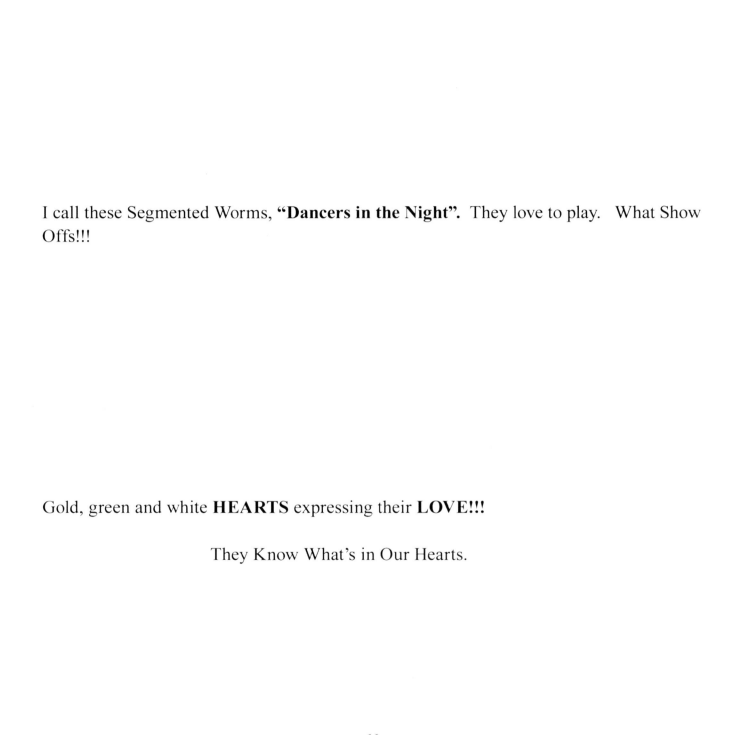

Gold, green and white **HEARTS** expressing their **LOVE!!!**

       They Know What's in Our Hearts.

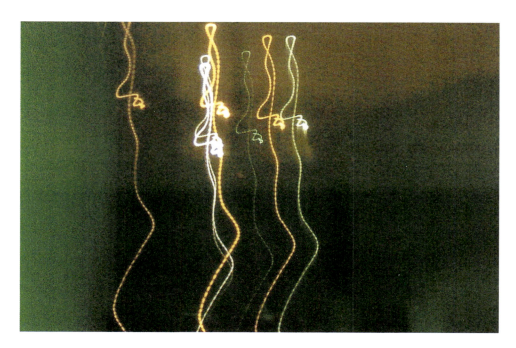

This Light Wave formation reminds me of a Praying Mantis. It's always fun to see what other people see in the formations.

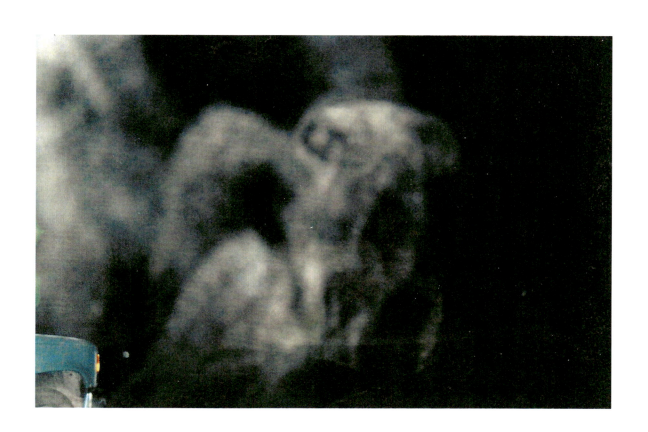

I was quite amazed when a couple of pictures showed this line from the sky to the ground. It appears that way in the picture, but we know it isn't really there. Or is the line really there and you and I exist in the illusion?

One psychic friend said it is a **Direct Line to Heaven**. Imagine being able to climb up and see for yourself.   **MIRACLES HAPPEN!!!**

I was patiently taking pictures in my front yard of this beautiful tree my late husband planted and suddenly a red Orb to the right caught my eye.

Continuously shooting pictures, I asked the Orb to go on top of the tree just to see if it would. **WOW!!!** Isn't this beautiful? Proving again that these Light Beings are able to hear your thoughts and will comply, if they are in a good mood.

Last August 22nd my dear cat Bubba disappeared. He had been getting old, 17 years in fact, and I knew he had gone away to die. I looked all over for him just hoping to at least bring him home to bury. But I couldn't find him. He was always around me when I worked outside, such a loving sweetheart. On the evening of the 24th – two days after he left, I asked him if at all possible would he please come through in the pictures so I would know he was still alive and well.

Never before had I gotten a picture of anything like this – pure white energy with a **tail sticking out**. I knew right away this was my beloved Bubba and that this was his way of letting me know it was truly him. Here he is sitting on my driveway out front where he sat many nights before. **God Bless little guy.**

That same night a few hours later after Bubba showed up for me, I took this picture. It looks like an Angel. Could it be little Bubba coming back to be my **Angel of Protection?**

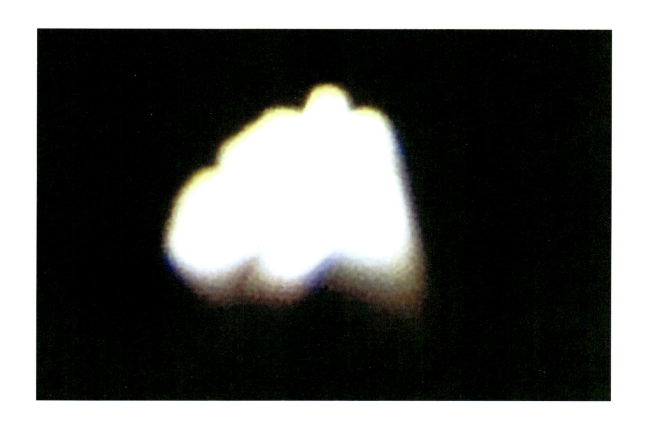

Closing Thoughts

Do we live on after physical death? Absolutely! No doubt in my mind. One theory is that at death when the soul leaves the body, it comes out as a sphere (Orb) and goes back to its soul group. Then, in time, each one in the soul group decides if they are to reincarnate and which role they will play next time around. One may choose to be the husband, wife, mother or father, others may choose to be children or friends – taking on whatever role will help them achieve their soul purpose in the next carnation. Interesting concept.

When souls go to the other side, they are not limited like we are here on Earth. Though maybe we are only limited because we have established that belief pattern and have not yet realized our full potential.

People that have had near death experiences (NDEs), speak of extraordinary happenings while on the other side. They realize that life exists after life on Earth and that our goal is to learn unconditional love for all life with the realization we are all ONE, no One being better than anyone else. Quantum Mechanics now has proven we are all of the same energy - we are all connected.

I think the idea is to respect all forms of life from the beautiful loving Angel of Light to the hard working ant or the poor little beetle struggling to turn back over after landing on its back so it can go about its business, doing whatever beetles do. As the late David Hawkins said in his "Discovery" cds, when One becomes more Enlightened, he makes sure he doesn't step on the beetle and if it is lying on its back, he reaches down and flips it over, right side up. How many of us take the time to do that? Isn't there a spark of God in all life?

A good friend of mine who had lost her husband asked if I would take pictures at his funeral. The pictures taken in the church show there is one Orb on the wall above his picture and in a few other pictures taken that day confirming he was there at the funeral with her, never leaving her side.

At the recent funeral for my sister in law, one Orb appeared above her picture sitting on the table. In another photo there was an Orb just below the ceiling. She was also there at her own funeral. They never really leave us, only physically. Love is energy and never dies.

I have so many more pictures to show that I did not have room for in this book, including some Fairies, beautiful Sun photos and an actual Soul Group, thanks to my dear cousin that passed in 2012. New Beings come along all the time and Orbs with faces and many interesting patterns and colors. Some may be Spirits with the Orb being the vehicle for travel, others are Nature Spirits and possibly even Aliens. I don't think they all need a space ship to travel inter-dimensionally.

What else could be lurking out there in the night sky just waiting to get its picture taken? My camera is ready to capture whatever may come its way.

God Bless!!!

Author Bio

Angelique Patrice resides in Washington where she worked and raised her two children. In the mid 80's she lived in France for three years and shortly after returning to the states, met and married her soul mate. After his passing in 2006 while grieving her loss, photographing Orbs and other Inter-dimensional Beings became her passion. It was her fascination with "Spirit Beings" that lifted her up out of her depression bringing her to the realization that all life is energy and never really dies. It just changes form.

Other interests include Quantum Physics, Consciousness, Near Death Experiences (NDE's), other realms of existence, and energy healing. Along with Metaphysics, she has studied Reiki, Pranic Healing and Matrix Energetics. ***"Angelic Luminosities"*** is her first book and she is presently working on another.

CPSIA information can be obtained
at www.ICGtesting.com
Printed in the USA
BVXC01n2002070414
350007BV00001B/1